Animals and Us

PITREAVIE PRIMARY SCHOOL

Claire Llewellyn

OXFORD
UNIVERSITY PRESS

OXFORD
UNIVERSITY PRESS

Great Clarendon Street, Oxford OX2 6DP

Oxford University Press is a department of the University of Oxford.
It furthers the University's objective of excellence in research, scholarship,
and education by publishing worldwide in

Oxford   New York

Auckland   Cape Town   Dar es Salaam   Hong Kong   Karachi
Kuala Lumpur   Madrid   Melbourne   Mexico City   Nairobi
New Delhi   Shanghai   Taipei   Toronto

With offices in

Argentina   Austria   Brazil   Chile   Czech Republic   France   Greece
Guatemala   Hungary   Italy   Japan   Poland   Portugal   Singapore
South Korea   Switzerland   Thailand   Turkey   Ukraine   Vietnam

Oxford is a registered trade mark of Oxford University Press
in the UK and in certain other countries

British Library Cataloguing in Publication Data

Data available

ISBN 978-0-19-919885-6

9 10

Printed in China by Imago

Acknowledgements

The publisher would like to thank the following for permission to reproduce
photographs: **p4** NHPA/B & C Alexander, **p5**b Photolibrary/Edward Parker, t
Photolibrary/Gordon Garradd, **p6**b Alamy/FLPA, t Photolibrary/OSF, **p7**t Photolibrary/Science
Pictures Ltd, b Photolibrary/OSF, **p10**b NHPA/Stephen Dalton, r Corbis/Yann Arthus-Bertrand,
l Photolibrary/Konrad Wothe, **p11**t Nature Picture Library/Mike Read, r NHPA/Daniel Heuchlin,
p13t FLPA/Roger Tidman, b FLPA/Heidi & Hans-Jeurgen Koch/Minden Pictures, **p15** NHPA/Hellio
& Van Ingen, **p16** NHPA/Stephen Dalton, **p17** Alamy, **p19**l Alamy, r NHPA/Ernie James, **p20**
Classet/OUP, **p21** FLPA/David T Grewcock, **p23**l Alamy/Jack Sullivan, b Nature Picture /Phil
Savoie, r Photolibrary/Mike Hill, **p24**l Nature Picture Library/Michael Durham, r FLPA/Roel
Hoeve/Foto Natura, **p25**t Photolibrary/David Cayless, b Nature Picture Library/Georgette
Douwma, **p27**l FLPA, r NHPA/B & C Alexander, **p28**l NHPA/Martin Harvey, t NHPA/Joe Blossom,
r Photolibrary, b NHPA/Daniel Heuchlin, **p30** Photolibrary/William Gray

Cover: Alamy/David Jones

All illustrations by Graham Smith except **p12** Roger Gorringe

CONTENTS

A shared world

Human beings have lived on Earth for many thousands
of years. During this time, our lives have been linked
with those of other living things.

Shared needs

Early people and animals had very
similar needs. They both needed food
and shelter to survive. They both
needed protection from **predators**.
Some animals lived in groups, just as
humans do. With such similar needs, it
is not surprising that in some cases
animals and humans became partners
in the struggle to survive. At times,
humans needed animals; at times, it
was the other way round.

Adapt and survive

To form relationships with one
another, animals and people
adapted their behaviour; they
lived in new places, ate different
kinds of food and tried new ways
of doing things. This book looks at
humans and animals: it examines
how relationships between them
developed. It also looks at some of
the benefits and the costs to them.

From earliest times, people benefited from animals. We used their bones to make tools, their skins to make tents and their furs to keep us warm.

Animals and humans get different benefits from their relationship with one another. Can you say which side of the partnership is benefiting in these pictures?

Close to home

Animals have always lived in our sheltered, comfortable homes. They burrow deep in the fibres of our carpets and rugs. They hide in soft mattresses and pillows. They scurry among the clothes in our wardrobes and drawers. Most of the animals that live in our homes are so tiny that they are invisible to the naked eye. They are **scavengers** and **parasites**. The scavengers feed on anything they find. The parasites feed on us!

Scavengers

Scavengers moved in with us when people first sheltered in caves, over 30,000 years ago. They burrowed into the furs and skins people wore to keep out the cold.

The clothes moth lays its eggs in our clothes. When its grubs hatch out, they feed on wool, leaving tell-tale holes.

The furniture beetle lays its eggs on our wooden furniture and beams. Its tiny grubs, known as woodworm, make small round holes in the wood.

Parasites

Parasites are pesky creatures that live and feed on other animals. Some parasites survive on people without us even noticing them; but others, such as dustmites and mosquitoes, cause huge problems with our health.

The **microscopic** dustmite feeds on the dry dead **cells** that brush off our skin every day. At night, there are probably millions of the creatures feasting inside the mattress on our bed. Next morning, as we shake our bedding, the dustmites' cast-off skins and dead bodies often make us sneeze. They can even trigger asthma attacks.

The mosquito injects its sharp mouthparts into a blood **capillary** under our skin. It gets a juicy meal of blood; we get an itchy bite.

Our best friend

Dogs and people have a very special partnership and live side by side. Dogs are fun and loyal friends, but they also protect us and our property and help us in many different ways. In return, dogs enjoy food, shelter and human companionship.

The dog's distant **ancestor** is the wolf. How did such a fierce animal ever come to live in our homes?

From the wolf to the dog

About 15,000 years ago:

A lost, hungry wolf cub visited humans in a cave.

The cub was fed and petted.

At night, it slept by the fire. It barked at any sign of danger.

The wolf-dog helped people when they hunted.

The animal had cubs of its own. The **docile** ones were allowed to stay. Any savage ones were turned away.

Over the generations, the animals became tamer. They lived with people now.

Breeding dogs

Humans saw that individual dogs had useful **characteristics**.
Some were intelligent and easily trained. Some were good at
hunting. Others were small enough to go down holes. Dogs with
these useful characteristics were bred with one another. This
resulted in the dog breeds we know today.

Which breed is which?

Look at the pictures of the dogs below.
Can you match each one to its description?

1 intelligent and easy to train
2 a small but ferocious rat-catcher
3 strong and able to withstand the cold

(See answers below.)

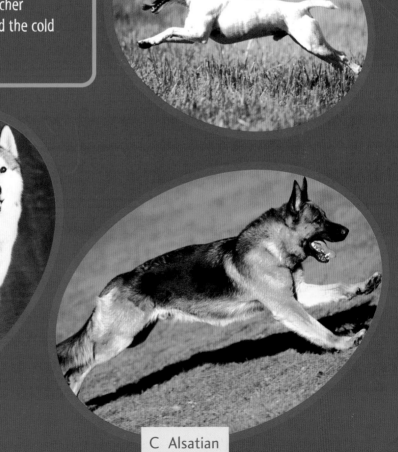

B Jack Russell

A Husky

C Alsatian

Answers: 1C; 2B; 3A

The lodgers

Many animals make use of our homes and buildings. Every summer, swifts and swallows perch on walls, beams and under house **eaves** to make their nests. Bats **hibernate** in attics and cellars. Owls roost in barns. Geckos, a type of tropical lizard, crawl over ceilings and walls, feeding on their insect prey.

All these animals used to nest in the wild, and some of their kind still do. Swifts, swallows and bats nested in caves. Owls and geckos sheltered in trees. Over many thousands of years, these animals adapted to human buildings and sheltered somewhere new.

Storks often build their nests on the chimneys of houses.

Fruit bats like to shelter in quiet, warm places.

Swallows build their mud nests on the walls of houses, barns and churches, under the overhanging eaves.

Who benefits?

When animals live alongside humans, both sides can benefit.
Look at the benefits in the chart below.

Benefits	human benefit	animal benefit
① Shelter from the weather		✔
② Lots of flies to eat		✔
③ Lots of mice to eat		✔
④ Fewer flies buzzing around	✔	
⑤ Able to raise more young		✔
⑥ Fewer mice raiding the food	✔	

Clever creatures

Geckos can walk upside-down on the ceiling thanks to the tiny hairs on their feet, which give them a velcro-like grip. These lizards have learned to hunt near lights, which attract their insect prey.

The pigeon: hero or pest?

For thousands of years, pigeons have lived alongside people. This partnership has had its ups and downs. The bird's ability to return to its home made it valuable in times of war. But the pigeons that **pollute** our cities and towns are nothing but pests!

The hero

Pigeons have a natural homing instinct and always return to their roosts at night. During World Wars I (1914–18) and II (1939–45), specially-trained birds known as 'carrier pigeons' were used to carry secret information.

The birds were housed in military roosts.

Pigeons were taken on planes, ships, and submarines. They were released to get help when people were in danger.

Some birds carried tiny cameras that took pictures of enemy ships and troops.

Many pigeons were awarded medals for bravery. There are even memorials to those that that died.

The pest

Millions of pigeons live in our town centres. Pigeons know that wherever people live, there is food to be found.

Pigeons nest on any available ledge and peck at rubbish and crumbs.

Pigeon droppings ruin buildings, statues and benches. They carry **bacteria** that spread disease.

Every year we spend huge sums of money cleaning and protecting buildings, and unblocking gutters and drains.

Crop raiders

Have you or your family tried growing your own food? If you have, you will know that a lot of it is eaten before you can even pick it. From slugs and snails to rabbits and deer, our animal neighbours take their share. When animals start destroying farm crops it can be a serious battle. Many farmers use **pesticides**. While these powerful chemicals kill insect pests, they can be harmful to other creatures and to human health.

WANTED!
Dead or Alive

Rook

Colorado beetle
(potatoes)

Carrot fly
(carrot)

Cabbage-white butterfly
(cabbage)

Wood pigeon

Have you seen these crop-raiders?

Swarms of locusts

Locusts are large grasshoppers that live in warm parts of the world. In some years, millions of them gather in **swarms**, and eat a whole region's crops. This leaves people with little to eat. Locusts are not a recent problem. A Bible story tells how a plague of locusts **devastated** Ancient Egypt. Many countries in northern Africa still battle with locusts today.

Locusts threaten 1m with famine

Ibrahima Sylla
in Nouakchott

Nearly a million people in west Africa face famine unless they get international aid to battle swarms of locusts devouring their crops in the region's worst plague in 15 years, farmers and experts warned.

Locusts were in the headlines in 2004 when they were expected to destroy 80% of the **cereal** crop in some West African countries.

Food thieves

Sugar, flour, raisins, biscuits, bread – what food do you have in the cupboards at home? This and lots of other dried food is sometimes stolen by animal thieves, such as beetles, cockroaches and mice. Foodstore pests cause huge expense. They invade kitchens, warehouses, restaurants and shops, destroying 15 per cent of all the food that is intended for humans!

Gruesome twosome

Flour beetles and cockroaches are two major food pests. Would you want them laying eggs in your food?

Name: Flour beetle
Size: 3 mm long
Description: narrow, reddish-brown body
Feeds on: cereals, grains, beans, peas, dried fruits
Found in: boxes and bags of food
Danger: contaminates food

Name: Cockroach
Size: 9–14 mm long
Description: dark brown, flat, shiny body with long antennae
Feeds on: anything
Found in: kitchens, bakeries, drains
Danger: contaminates food, causes allergic reaction and spreads disease

Cat and mouse

Mice once lived and fed in the wild, but as soon as people began to store food, mice began to steal it. This was a problem in Ancient Egypt, where mice raided the granaries. Fortunately, wild cats were attracted by the mice and moved into human settlements. The Egyptians admired the cats for their beauty and hunting skills, and encouraged them to stay. This was the beginning of our **domestication** of the cat.

Cats are one of our most popular pets. Which side of the partnership benefits the most? Humans or animals?

Rats!

Rats are one of the world's most common animals and one of the most hated. To many people, just the thought of a rat's hunched back, damp fur, and long tail makes them shudder. The rat has become a symbol of evil in horror films and stories. Why is the rat such a hated figure? What secrets are hidden in its past?

6000 years of the rat

About 4000 BC
Rats live in the Far East, feeding on wild rice. As farmers begin to cultivate rice, rats feed on human foodstores. Their population increases rapidly.

About 3000 BC – AD 1300
Rats spread west to Ancient Greece and Europe. They raid and contaminate food stores.

Animal puzzle

Q: How fast can rats breed?

A: Female rats produce six to eight young every three or four weeks. At that rate, in a single year, two rats and their offspring can produce a thousand new rats!

1347–51
A disease called the 'bubonic plague', or the 'Black Death', spreads through Europe, killing 25 million people. It is thought to have been spread by rat's fleas.

Present day
Rats live in every city and town and their population probably equals humans. They damage and contaminate foodstuffs and buildings, and spread diseases.

1500–1700
In the age of the great explorers, rats stow away on ships and are transported around the world. In many countries they kill off native birds and other animal species.

On the farm

For about 10,000 years people have reared animals for food. Today's farm animals – cows, sheep, chickens and goats – have all descended from wild animals in a process known as 'domestication'. How did it begin?

Domesticating animals

As the first farmers grew crops like wheat and barley, the wild sheep and goats found them irresistible. Some of these animals were tamer than others. When people offered them food, shelter and protection from predators, they were tempted to stay. The animals grew quickly and gave birth to healthy young. The weakest animals were killed for food. Domestication had begun. But which animals were suited to this kind of life? As it turned out, surprisingly few.

So you want to be domesticated...

Not all animals are suitable for domestication.

Do you have the following characteristics?

Value to humans
- must provide food, materials or labour

Diet
- **herbivores** preferred, as they are safer and easier to feed

Growth
- must grow quickly

Breeding
- must breed easily in captivity

Calmness
- must not panic when startled

Temperament
- must be easy to control

Social structure
- must enjoy company and follow a leader

Domesticated animals descended from wild animals that are now endangered or **extinct**:

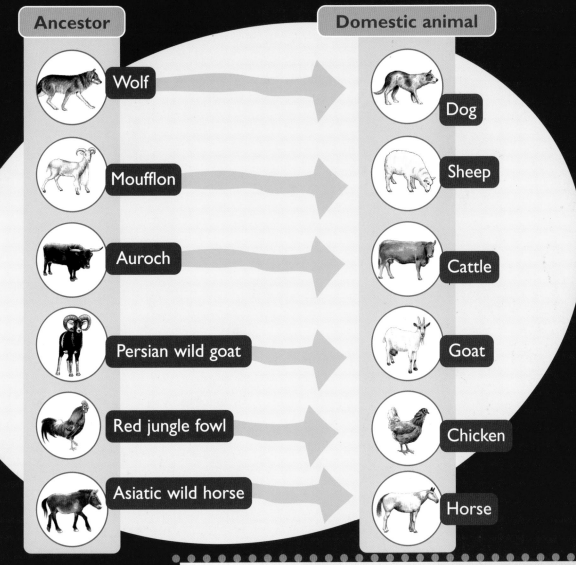

Ancestor	Domestic animal
Wolf	Dog
Moufflon	Sheep
Auroch	Cattle
Persian wild goat	Goat
Red jungle fowl	Chicken
Asiatic wild horse	Horse

Farming animals provides us with a constant supply of fresh food, wool and other materials. Only a small number of people are needed to work on farms, leaving the rest of the population with time to do other useful things.

Horse power

Have you ever ridden a horse? If you have then you will know that there is a special relationship between a rider and a horse. The first people ever to ride wild horses must have had a lot of time and patience. With something unfamiliar on its back, a horse's instinct would have been to panic, buck wildly and run away. But by around 2000 BC, people were much more experienced with animals, and they learned to gain horses' trust.

Domestication of the horse

25,000 BC
Large herds of wild horses graze on the grasslands of Europe and Asia. Our ancestors hunt them for food.

2000 BC
People begin to ride on horseback. Soon horses are being used for exploration and warfare.

3500 BC
People in Asia begin to herd wild horses. For the next 5000 years, horse power is the main form of transport for people and goods.

About AD 1900
The horse gives way to the motor car and the railway as the main form of transport.

On the back of a horse

People and horses work together in many different ways. Horses have been bred this way to do different jobs, such as ranch work, police work, and for activities, such as horse racing.

Clever creatures

Zebras, a member of the horse family, could never be tamed. They have such wide vision they could not be **lassoed**. They also have a vicious bite!

Animal puzzle

Q: Why do riders always groom their horse?

A: Horses often groom one another as a sign of friendship. By copying this behaviour, riders are strengthening their own friendship with the horse.

Life in the city

In recent centuries, the world's population has grown enormously. Instead of living in small villages, most people live in cities and towns, which swallow up more and more land. The **urban environment** is difficult for animals – with its concrete, traffic, noise and lights – but some have managed to adapt to the change.

Easy pickings

Cities are packed with houses, hotels, restaurants and bars. Their rubbish bins contain fish heads, bones and half-eaten chops – easy pickings for hungry animals. In different parts of the world, foxes, raccoons and even polar bears are known to raid city bins.

A warmer roost

Cities are warmer than the surrounding countryside and the buildings give off heat. As a result, huge numbers of starlings and other birds fly into the city to roost. Birds of prey have followed them there. Sparrowhawks and falcons nest on high-rise tower blocks, swooping on smaller birds as they gather for the night.

Seagulls that once fed on the coast now feed on rubbish tips in cities and towns.

Clever creatures

In a Japanese city, crows have found a clever way to break open walnuts. They wait beside traffic lights, holding a nut in their beak. When the lights turn red, the crows fly down and place the nuts on the road. The cars move forward, crushing the nuts, and when the traffic stops again, the crows collect the kernels.

In winter wild geese and ducks shelter in parks, where the temperature is a degree or two warmer.

A foxy move

The fox has had a difficult relationship with people. For centuries it has been shot by farmers protecting their chickens, and hunted for sport and its fur. The fox has moved from the country to cities and towns, and its luck is beginning to change.

Urban benefits

Foxes are clever animals. They have learned that cities make excellent homes. There are plenty of safe, sheltered spots – garages, sheds and railway sidings – where foxes can live and raise their young. Best of all there are thousands of people who provide a year-round supply of food.

What do they eat?

Insects, birds, berries and mice – **rural** foxes eat many kinds of food. Do urban foxes eat the same kind of diet? How much do they scavenge from bins? 600 dead urban foxes had their stomach contents examined to see exactly what they ate. This showed that city pickings were a big part of a fox's diet.

earthworms

pets

scavenged food

wild animals

plant food

insects

About one third of the food found in foxes' stomachs was made up of city pickings.

Pest or guest?

In Britain, people are divided about the fox: some people see it as a pest and enjoy hunting it with dogs; others admire the handsome fox and believe hunting is cruel. These people are locked in an angry debate. In the meantime, foxes are thriving in cities.

For:

" The fox is a beautiful animal. "

Against:

" Foxes are killers: they kill chickens, lambs, ducks and cats. "

" Foxes breed quickly. They soon outnumber and kill other local animals. "

" It's great to watch foxes in the garden. "

" Foxes are useful. They kill rats, mice and other harmful pests. "

" In some countries, foxes carry rabies, a deadly disease. That could happen here. "

Animal puzzle

Q: Do urban foxes live longer lives?

A: No. Most urban foxes die before they are three years old. More than half of them are killed by cars.

Animals in danger

As the human population grows, wild animals and humans are squeezed closer together. In many parts of the world, animals' natural **habitats** are being cleared to make room for building or farming. Some kinds of animals can adapt to these changes and live side-by-side with people. But most of them face problems. They do not have enough space to live. They cannot find enough food. These problems mean fewer and fewer of them survive. The animals on this page are all endangered. Could they become extinct?

Endangered!

Name: Goliath frog

Habitat: fast-flowing rainforest rivers

Distribution: equatorial Africa

Problems: habitat loss due to logging, farming and the building of dams. Hunted for food and the pet trade

Endangered!

Name: Mountain gorilla

Habitat: tropical cloud forests

Distribution: central Africa

Problems: forest habitat has been cleared for timber and to make way for farms, mines and roads

Endangered!

Name: Kakapo

Habitat: forest and scrubland

Distribution: islands off New Zealand

Problems: hunted almost to the point of extinction by dogs, cats, rats and other predators introduced by human settlers

The future?

During the last 50 years, scientists and **conservationists** have been working together to protect endangered animals. They have been studying animals to learn about their needs, setting up wildlife parks and reserves, and organising breeding programmes. They have persuaded many governments to ban hunting and protect important habitats. This is a new partnership with animals – one that ensures their survival. Their future lies in our hands.

These young orang-utans are orphans, growing up on a wildlife reserve.

What can I do?

You can help endangered animals by joining an organization such as the *Worldwide Fund for Nature WWF.* You can also join local wildlife groups to conserve habitats near your home.

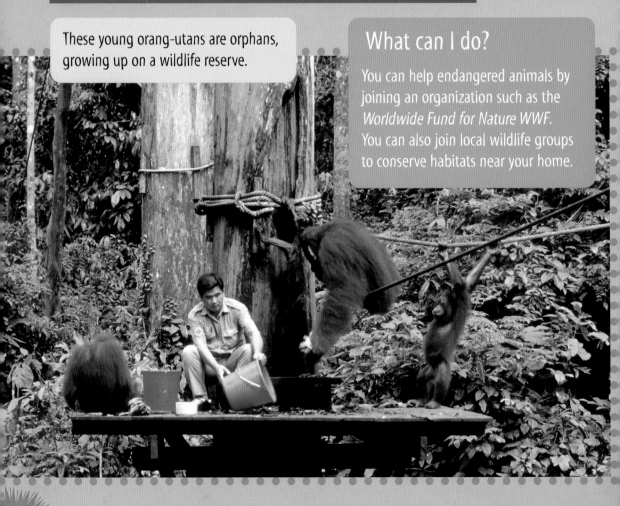

Glossary

adapt – to change in order to fit a new situation

ancestor – an early type of animal which lived a long time ago, and is related to animals of the same kind today

bacteria – microscopic living things, some of which cause disease

capillary – the smallest blood vessels in the body, some of which lie close to the surface of the skin

cell – the smallest building blocks of the body

cereals – plants, such as wheat and oats, whose seeds provide us with grain

characteristic – a special and easily recognized quality of something

conservationist – a scientist who specialises in the protection of the natural world

contaminate – to spoil and infect

devastate – to completely destroy

docile – easy to control

domestication – the taming of animals so that they learn to live with humans, under our control

eaves – the overhanging edge of a roof

environment – everything in the world around us, on land and in the air and sea

extinct – no longer living on the Earth

habitat – the place where an animal naturally lives

herbivore – an animal that eats plants

hibernate – to spend the winter in a deep sleep

lasso – a rope with a noose, used for catching horses and cattle

microscopic – so small that it can only be seen with a microscope

parasite – a plant or animal that lives on or inside another living thing and obtains food from it

pesticide – chemicals that are used by farmers and gardeners to destroy pests

pollute – to make dirty and unhealthy

predator – an animal that kills other animals for food

rural – of the countryside

scavenger – an animal that feeds on dead animals and waste

swarm – a huge number of insects flying together

urban – of the city

Index